Pass Your Exam

Sara Miller McCune founded SAGE Publishing in 1965 to support the dissemination of usable knowledge and educate a global community. SAGE publishes more than 1000 journals and over 800 new books each year, spanning a wide range of subject areas. Our growing selection of library products includes archives, data, case studies and video. SAGE remains majority owned by our founder and after her lifetime will become owned by a charitable trust that secures the company's continued independence.

Los Angeles | London | New Delhi | Singapore | Washington DC | Melbourne

SUPER
QUICK
SKILLS

Pass Your Exam

Lorraine Anderson
Gordon Spark

SAGE

Los Angeles | London | New Delhi
Singapore | Washington DC | Melbourne

Los Angeles | London | New Delhi
Singapore | Washington DC | Melbourne

SAGE Publications Ltd
1 Oliver's Yard
55 City Road
London EC1Y 1SP

SAGE Publications Inc.
2455 Teller Road
Thousand Oaks, California 91320

SAGE Publications India Pvt Ltd
B 1/I 1 Mohan Cooperative Industrial Area
Mathura Road
New Delhi 110 044

SAGE Publications Asia-Pacific Pte Ltd
3 Church Street
#10-04 Samsung Hub
Singapore 049483

Editor: Jai Seaman
Assistant editor: Charlotte Bush
Production editor: Tanya Szwarnowska
Proofreader: Aud Scriven
Marketing manager: Catherine Slinn
Cover design: Shaun Mercier
Typeset by: C&M Digitals (P) Ltd, Chennai, India
Printed in the UK

Library of Congress Control Number: 2019953063

British Library Cataloguing in Publication data

A catalogue record for this book is available
from the British Library

ISBN 978-1-5297-1784-6

At SAGE we take sustainability seriously. Most of our products are printed in the UK using responsibly
sourced papers and boards. When we print overseas we ensure sustainable papers are used as measured
by the PREPS grading system. We undertake an annual audit to monitor our sustainability

Contents

Everything in this book!

Section 1   What can I expect in my exams?

Exams come in lots of different shapes and sizes. This section will introduce some of the more common formats and encourage you to think about the different demands they may present.

Section 2   I'm stressed by the thought of exams. What can I do?

Exam stress is common. In this section, we recognize it as a normal part of the process and think about some of the ways you can keep the nerves under control.

Section 3   What's the best way to approach preparing for my exams?

Getting organized is the first step on the road to revising effectively. This section covers some of the basics of revision timetabling and highlights a couple of important concepts which can make a real difference to your planning.

Section 4 I can't get down to revision. What should I do?

In this section, we tackle the issue of procrastination head-on, helping you to identify the things that distract you and suggesting some common strategies for getting into the action habit.

Section 5 My previous revision techniques haven't worked. What can I do?

Many people develop revision techniques which are largely ineffective, especially at university level. This section shines a light on these common – but ineffective – techniques and introduces you to some scientifically proven alternative revision approaches.

Section 6 My exam is today. What should I do?

Exam day can be a particularly stressful experience. This section looks at a number of steps you can take to stay on top of things before, during and after the exam.

Section 7 I've got resits. What should I do now?

Resits are not the end of the world. This section will help you frame such situations much more positively and to view any resits you may have as an opportunity rather than a threat.

Section 8 My exams are over. What next?

Once the exams are over it's natural to want to forget all about them and move on. But a little reflection at this point can help you go into future exams with increased confidence. This section will help you to do just that.

What can I expect in my exams?

10 second summary

Exams come in all shapes and sizes and it's important you understand the format(s) for your exams – there should be no surprises.

60 second summary

Exams are a game. Once you understand the rules, you know how to play that game to win.

The first thing you need to find out is what type of exam you will be sitting. Exams are all different – many exams are done online but some may still be handwritten. Depending on the subjects you're studying your exams might involve writing essays or short answers, completing multiple choice quizzes, or carrying out calculations.

Once you know what type of exam you'll be sitting you can develop the most effective techniques for preparing for, tackling, and passing that type of exam. This section will help you understand a range of possible exam scenarios.

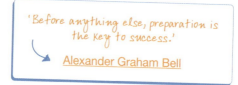

'Before anything else, preparation is the key to success.'

Alexander Graham Bell

All shapes and sizes

One of the key considerations in how you approach thinking about how to pass your exam should be the type of exam(s) you will face. Don't think about it as 'one size fits all', avoid approaching the exam in the same way regardless of the fact you may be faced with a variety of exam styles. Here are some examples to think about.

Essay-based exams

Although they are becoming less fashionable in some subjects, essay questions remain the most common type of exam that you might face. Why is this?

- Exams allow universities to examine lots of students at the same time and in the same place.

- The format is popular because it allows examiners to test the breadth and depth of your knowledge and understanding, rather than just testing your memory.

If you face essay-based exams then the chances are you've also had to write essays as part of your coursework for the same module. There are some differences, however, between coursework essays and exam essays which make the latter a bit more challenging.

Essay-based exam An exam where you will be required to write a defined number of properly structured essay answers.

The differences between coursework essays and exam essays

Have a go at listing what you think the differences are between coursework essays and exam essays. Then compare it with our points below.

....

....

....

....

....

....

....

....

....

Suggested answers:

- In an exam, you usually won't know what the specific questions are beforehand.
- You won't get the chance to research the questions before having to answer them.
- In an exam the main challenge you are up against is time.

Exams are often still handwritten. When was the last time you wrote solidly for a couple of hours? If you are likely to face this type of exam, your revision plan should include regular bouts of writing to allow you to become accustomed to working for that length of time.

There's one big danger with essay type exams – not answering the question. This is a very common mistake with this type of exam. To overcome it, try to break your question down using the following model:

Instruction	Topic	Focus	Restriction(s)
The critical task you're being asked to carry out	The general topic area	The specific element of the topic you're being asked to focus upon	Any other elements within the question which help you further narrow the focus

Here's an example:

Discuss the use of social media as a design tool in Higher Education.

Instruction	Topic	Focus	Restriction(s)
Discuss	Social Media	Social media as a design tool	Higher education only

Now try it with one of your exam questions. You could use a question from a mock exam or a past paper.

Question:

....

Instruction	Topic	Focus	Restriction(s)

Breaking the question down like this will help ensure you are focused on answering the question, and not on regurgitating everything you've remembered about the topic from your revision.

Essay exams with a twist

If you have an open book exam don't be fooled into thinking that it will be easier than a traditional exam – challenges remain!

- You still won't know the questions beforehand.

- You'll be allowed to take course texts and, in some cases, notes into the exam with you.

- There will be strict conditions applied to the type of material you use – for example, you may not be allowed to use a textbook in which you have scribbled your own notes.

Open book exams can sound like a good thing but they can be problematic if your approach to revision is inadequate, so be on your guard. You can use up a lot of your valuable time searching for answers rather than thinking about them, so revision should be similar to that for a regular exam. See the open books as a bonus rather than as an excuse to scrimp on the preparation.

Open book exam An exam where you are allowed to refer to certain material (usually textbooks or notes).

Multiple choice question (MCQ) exams

Some general pointers:

- MCQ exams can be paper-based or online.

Many science-based subjects in particular create online MCQ exams; sometimes you may even be able to take these tests several times as part of your learning process.

- Different questions will be generated every time from a database of questions.

The more sophisticated approaches will provide short responses on why your answer was right or wrong.

- There is no right or wrong technique in terms of approaching an MCQ exam.

Many people like to go through the paper quickly, answering all the questions they know as swiftly as possible, before going back over the remaining questions and taking more time to work out the most likely answer. Others prefer to work through each question chronologically. The key is to practise and to come up with an approach that works for you.

Multiple choice questions (MCQs) A common type of exam where you are given a question and a series of possible answers, from which you must choose the correct response. Likely to involve answering a large number of questions in a relatively short space of time.

- It's important that you manage your time and make sure you get through all the questions.

Whatever your strategy, your first priority should be to never run out of time. Indeed, it's best to leave yourself a little time to review your answers.

☐ Find out what kind of exam(s) you'll be sitting.

☐ Understand what to expect from each type of exam.

☐ Tailor your revision approach to the type(s) of exam you'll face.

☐ Use past papers or sample questions so that you can understand and practise the style of questions that are used in your subject area.

☐ Read the other sections in this book for more practical tips on revising for and sitting your exams.

A student told us

'If you've got an MCQ exam, unless you're pretty sure you made a mistake with an answer, go with your first instinct.'

I'm stressed by the thought of exams. What can I do?

10 second summary

Being anxious about your exams is OK! Taking an organized approach to your revision can help control these feelings – and possibly even channel them to your benefit.

It's perfectly normal to feel nervous about exams. In fact, it would be strange if you didn't! But you can work on approaching your exams with a more positive mindset so that they become a less scary thought. You've already started by reading this book which aims to equip you with

- tips

- ideas

- practical strategies

that will allow you to approach exams with confidence. Not convinced yet? OK, think about it as a 3-step 'confidence developing' process. If you have confidence

1   in how you **plan** your revision

2   in how you **carry out** your revision

3   in the strategies you **develop** for tackling the exam itself

then you'll start to see exams as an opportunity rather than a threat, making them a much more positive prospect.

Fight or flight?

Most people are familiar with the fight or flight response – that instinctive reaction that allowed our ancestors to know whether to stand and fight the sabre-toothed tiger or to turn around and leg it. We still use it today, but because the threats we face are generally much less life-threatening than the example above, the triggering of that response can often cause harmful levels of stress to build up in our bodies.

'Taking control of a stressful situation is the first step to overcoming it.'

That's what happens to a lot of people when they're faced with exams and revision. The flight impulse kicks in and in the process fires a number of chemical changes in the body which are designed to help you flee the threat. But because there isn't any actual fleeing from exams, the process keeps building and building and building, making you more anxious and leading to further triggering of the flight impulse. It's a vicious circle.

Armed with the techniques from this book, and bolstered by a positive attitude, you really have no reason to fear exams – so you can reduce those feelings.

So here's an idea – don't flee, fight. See your exams as an opponent – a worthy opponent but also one that you can deal with. Forget fleeing. Face the ball, the game is on!

Take control

The first step towards fighting rather than fleeing is to be able to recognize the nature of the task before you, and to come up with a plan of action for meeting that task. Whilst the amount of material you need to cover and the challenge of the exams at the end of it all might fill you with dread or a sense of being overwhelmed, there are ways of tackling and overcoming the challenge.

Complete the following steps:

 Make a list of all the things you think you need to do in your revision – sometimes we can feel 'paralysed' by the volume of work we feel we have to do. Identifying these tasks, writing them down, and prioritising them can really help to put you back in control.

 Now take a few moments to list all the **positive** *things you've achieved to date* – we have a tendency to be self-critical and to see only the challenges we face. Learning to recognize the good things and adopt a more positive outlook can be a very powerful step in the right direction.

What do you already know about the subjects you need to study (it's almost certainly more than you think)? What kind of positive feedback have you had on coursework that you can build upon in your revision? What positive experiences do you have of passing exams in the past? It's important to remember when beginning the revision process that you're not starting from scratch!

Have you started to organize your study timetable? The ultimate practical step in taking back control and managing the workload, you can find advice and practical tips on how to do this in Section 3 of this book.

Keep that good feeling going by ticking things off as you go – feeling a real sense of progress in any big or long-term task is a strong motivating factor in helping us keep going with that task, so celebrate these landmarks and score things out of your timetable as you get through them.

Be open-minded and at least give some of these ideas a go. They have proved successful for many other people in various walks of life, including many students before you who have faced up to their exams.

It really is important that you maintain as positive an attitude as possible throughout the revision process. So, have you listed your progress to date? Feeling good? Great, you're ready to approach the revision process with newfound confidence.

Personal reflection

- Jot down a few words or thoughts about how the exam and revision process makes you feel.

- Now note how many of these words are negative. Can you turn them into a positive? For example, if you've written 'exams make me nervous' could you instead frame it as 'exams fill me with nervous excitement'? Or instead of worrying that you'll fail, reframe the exam as an opportunity to demonstrate your good progress.

- Write down a few practical things you could do to feel more in control of the process. You may wish to look again at the tips in this section, and return to this exercise when you've finished reading the whole book.

- Close your eyes and visualize your revision and exams going really well. Make the pictures as vivid as possible – soak up that good feeling you get from just knowing you're on top of it all.

- Try to maintain this positive vocabulary and imagery as you continue to revise for and sit your exams. When you feel yourself slipping back into negativity, try to quickly reframe things in a more positive manner.

A student told us

'Instead of stressing about exams I picture everything going really well. It's made a huge difference.'

What's the best way to approach preparing for my exams?

10 second summary

By being organized and having a clear sense of what you're trying to achieve, you can get the most out of the time available to you for exam preparation.

Having a clear a plan and knowing what you're trying to achieve can help you approach your revision in an organized and confident way. Getting started early, managing the time available to you, and setting clear goals all contribute towards exam success.

Creating a revision timetable that works for you can ensure you cover all the necessary material, give you a sense of progress, and help you avoid distractions and time wasting. This section will equip you with some tools and strategies to get your revision into shape!

'Putting together a revision timetable helped me organize my thoughts and prioritize the areas I really needed to focus on.'

Effective planning

Just as athletes carefully plan their training schedules in order to arrive at the big event in peak condition, so you can have a clear revision plan which helps you reach the day of the exam as well-prepared as possible.

Here are our **Top 5 Tips** for putting together an Olympic-class revision schedule:

1   *Work back from the date of your exams* – obvious, right? Yeah, so obvious that lots of people don't do it, and suddenly realize that they're running out of time to cover everything. So get the dates in there as soon as possible, so that you know the deadlines you're working towards.

2   *Be realistic* – about outside commitments, about how much you can do in any one day, about how long you can work in any one sitting. Creating a detailed revision plan is easy. Creating a realistic revision plan that works in the real world is harder and requires reflection, honesty with yourself and a healthy dose of realism.

3   *Prioritize* – yes, you want to cover everything but identify your strengths and weaknesses and spend more time – much more time – on the latter. Your mission here is to pick up as many marks as possible, not to spend hours studying stuff you already know pretty well.

4   *Know yourself* – are you a morning person? A slow starter? A night owl? Whilst you almost certainly don't have the luxury of only working when you feel like it, you are free to schedule your day in such a way that you can focus on the more difficult tasks when you know you're at your sharpest. Be careful though – exams are never scheduled at 2 in the morning, so if you do prefer to burn the midnight oil, one of your aims should be to use the revision process to get used to working effectively during the day.

5   *Taper* – it's natural to build up the intensity of your revision as the exams approach, but try to schedule things so that you finish the heavy duty work with a few days or more to spare. In sports training this is known as tapering. Do you think athletes are training at full pelt the last few days before the Olympic Final? No, they've already put in the hard yards and are now just keeping things ticking over. That should be your goal too when it comes to exam revision.

> **Tapering** The practice of levelling off your revision as the exam approaches so that the last few days are spent reviewing learning rather than in intensive cramming.

'You can't change plans if you don't have a plan to begin with.'

Two key concepts

If you can take care of the practical points previously discussed, then you'll be well on the road to building an effective revision plan. But there are two slightly more advanced concepts which have been scientifically proven to improve the quality of your revision:

Spaced practice simply means spacing out the revision you do on any single topic. Research suggests that if you have allocated a set amount of time to study a particular topic, you will learn far more effectively if, rather than studying it all in one day, you divide that time up into shorter blocks and space these individual blocks out over several days or weeks.

Spaced practice This refers to the theory that time allocated to a specific topic will be more productive if split over several revision slots rather than completed in one sitting.

Interleaving goes hand in hand with spaced practice and refers to the idea that in any one individual study block, rather than focusing on one specific aspect of a topic, or a particular skill, we should mix up different aspects or skills into the one study session. For example,

Interleaving The practice of mixing up topics and revision activities within a single revision slot.

a medical student might do some questions on anatomy, watch a short video about immunology and refresh their reading on biochemistry, rather than looking at just one of these areas. In this way, they will begin to see the links between all the different elements of the course and engage with the material in a much deeper fashion than if they looked at each in isolation.

By combining spaced practice and interleaving with the practical tips from earlier in this section you can turbo charge your revision, putting you in the best shape possible to arrive at the exams primed for success.

How to build a timetable that *works*

1 Note down the dates of your exams.

2 Make a note of all your other commitments.

3 Work out how much time that leaves you to spend on each subject for which you have an exam.

4 Identify your strengths and weaknesses in each subject and prioritize areas you need to work on.

5 Now allocate topics to each of your study blocks, being realistic about how much you can achieve in one day and in any one sitting.

6 Spread topics out across your entire schedule (spaced practice) rather than in one big block.

7 Now detail what you want to cover in each sitting, being sure to mix up topics and activities (interleaving).

If you've followed the steps in this section you should be well on your way to having a powerful revision plan which is realistic, focused and effective and puts you firmly in control. Remember though that the plan is there to help you, not to constrain you. Don't be afraid to modify your plan as you go, in order to account for changing priorities, faster or slower than expected progress, and all the little interruptions that life tends to throw our way. We'll deal with some of these specific distractions, including the biggest one of all – procrastination – in the next section.

CHECK POINT How effective is your revision timetable?

Have you:

☐ Worked back from the date of your exams?

☐ Covered all the relevant material?

☐ Prioritized weaker areas?

☐ Spaced revision of specific topics out over several sessions?

☐ Ensured you take multiple approaches to the same topics?

☐ Timetabled breaks and time off?

Congratulations

So far, you've identified the types of exam you're going to face, thought about how you're going to handle the inevitable stress that comes with revising for exams, and put together a plan for how you're going to approach the revision process. You're ready to get started! Or are you... ?

I can't get down to revision. What should I do?

10 second summary

Getting started can often be the hardest part. But by getting into the action habit and finding the right environment you can quickly build up the momentum you need to tackle your planned revision.

60 second summary

It's one thing to have a plan for our revision, another thing altogether putting that plan into action. We often put off doing things we're not looking forward to, but fortunately there are a number of practical approaches you can take to overcome this problematic procrastination. This section will equip you with tools and techniques for doing just that.

It's not only about what you study, it's also important to think about where you study and to be realistic about what you can achieve in that time. Studying in the moment rather than worrying about the big picture, cutting out distractions, and finding an environment that works for you are all important steps towards revision success. With these things in place, you will be well positioned to make the most of your study time.

Overcoming procrastination

There are a number of reasons why we procrastinate.

1 We don't enjoy or look forward to the task.

2 We feel overwhelmed by the task at hand (hopefully our advice on planning your revision has made this one less of a problem).

3 Alternatively, we may feel we've already left a task too late.

4 There may be a fear of failure.

5 We may be too easily distracted.

Do you recognize any of these in yourself? Are there other reasons for procrastination that we haven't listed here? As we've already suggested, procrastination is a pretty common human trait – if you've a tendency to put things off at times then you're probably just a normal human being. But right now, you find yourself in the position of needing to make the most you possibly can of your revision time.

So let's look at some strategies that can help you get into the action habit…

Procrastination The habit of putting off or avoiding tasks you don't want to do. Particularly prevalent around exam revision time!

Go 'off grid' – we live in a hyper-connected world these days, and that can be bad news when you're trying to put in some effective study. So log out of the social media sites, put the phone on silent and watch your productivity go through the roof.

> **Going 'off the grid'** The practice of avoiding all distractions. Although particularly referring to turning off email and social media notifications, it can also refer to physically removing yourself from a particular environment in order to avoid human distractions.

Be antisocial – even if you can bring yourself to log out of everything, there is still the problem of other people distracting you. So whether you're working in the library or at home, put up the proverbial 'do not disturb' sign and insist on a little 'me' time. You can always catch up with everyone at lunchtime.

Declutter – ever wandered around the library at exam time? It's incredible how many folders, books and other resources people seem to need for a couple of hours of study. With all that material to wade through, it's little wonder they don't know where to begin. You should gather only the resources you need for that particular study slot.

> **Decluttering** The practice, when studying, of gathering only the materials you need for any one study session, rather than being surrounded by books and notes that you do not need at that particular moment.

Reward yourself – most people find it easier to study in relatively short bursts. Set your goals for that burst of study accordingly, and then promise yourself a reward when you're done. It needn't be anything fancy – perhaps a coffee, or maybe even ten minutes to check back in to cyberspace to see if anyone's noticed you were away.

ACTIVITY What makes you procrastinate?

Try this for one study session, or for a whole day, to help you identify the factors that distract you and cause you to procrastinate:

- Keep a notebook or sheet of paper handy.

- Every time you notice yourself getting distracted from the task at hand, jot down what it was that made you lose your concentration.

- At the end of your study session, analyse your list.

- Identify which are bad distractions (e.g. social media alerts) and which are potentially useful (e.g. stopping to think over the point you're studying).

- Construct an action plan to reduce or eliminate the negative distractions (e.g. turning off alerts and notifications, working in a quieter environment, etc.).

'Time flies – but you can be the pilot.'

Getting the environment right

How effective is your study space? If you can answer 'yes' to the following questions you're good to go. If some of them are a 'no', think about what you might be able to do to improve in that area:

- Do you find your study space a comfortable (but maybe not *too* comfortable) place in which to spend time?

- Do you have easy access to all the materials you need for that study period?

- Have you done everything you can to minimize potential distractions?

- Do you have enough room to work without feeling cramped or crowded out?

- Do you have space to get up and walk around during short breaks?

A student told us

'Getting my study environment right really helped me overcome my procrastination.'

Being realistic

If we feel a task is beyond our abilities, we can easily find ourselves demotivated and searching for excuses to avoid getting started. Be realistic in terms of what you hope to achieve from each chunk of revision and break larger tasks down into more manageable bites.

This is where a well-focused timetable helps. Be as detailed as possible, breaking down even a one or two hour session into smaller chunks with precisely defined tasks, and following the principles of spaced practice and interleaving (see Section 3).

The other important thing to remember is that we're not robots. No matter how carefully we manage our time, there will always be occasions where we slip up, or just can't get going. And that's OK – the important thing is to notice when that's happening and to try to get back on task as soon as possible.

Many students find it difficult to get started with their revision. Procrastination is a normal human trait, so don't be hard on yourself if you find yourself falling into that trap. The important thing is to recognize when it is happening and to get back on task as quickly as possible. Hopefully some of the tips we've provided in this section will help you do that.

CHECK POINT Are you ready to get down to some productive work?

Which of the following points can you put a tick mark against?

☐ I've identified some of the things that cause me to procrastinate.

☐ I've explored some of the suggested strategies for overcoming procrastination.

☐ I've created a workspace that is comfortable and easy to work in.

☐ I've broken my revision schedule down into realistic and achievable 'chunks'.

My previous revision techniques haven't worked. What can I do?

10 second summary

Sometimes, we revise in a way that is time consuming but not very effective. Fortunately, there are other techniques you can try to see what works for you.

60 second summary

The first step in becoming more effective in your revision is to reflect on how you've worked in the past and to recognize what has and hasn't worked for you. Even then, that alone might not be enough to get you through your exams. The greater demands of learning at university may call for new approaches.

In fact, a number of popular 'traditional' revision techniques have been shown to be inefficient. If you're basing your revision on these techniques, it's important that you recognize their limitations, and identify potentially more effective and efficient approaches. That's what we'll explore in this section.

Old habits die hard

Research has shown that many of the common revision techniques that we develop are actually pretty ineffective when we're working at the higher and more complex levels required at university.

Examples of common but ineffective approaches are:

- Memorising presentation slides.

- Re-writing lecture notes.

- Re-reading lecture notes.

- Copying out passages from books, journals or other sources.

- Reading, over and over, passages from books, journals or other sources.

- Highlighting notes or text.

These are ineffective as they are largely passive or inactive approaches to learning. The good news is that there are many active strategies which are more effective, more interesting and less time-consuming. We'll look at some of these in the rest of this section.

Active vs passive learning Active learning refers to revision techniques which require you to 'do' something with the material rather than simply re-reading or re-writing.

'To exist is to change, to change is to mature, to mature is to go on creating oneself endlessly.'

Henri Bergson

Total recall

What is recall?

Recall or information retrieval is simply the process of returning to subjects you have already studied over time to strengthen your understanding and memory retention. There's a lot of evidence to suggest that such an approach is much more beneficial compared to just ticking topics off as completed and never looking at them again.

Recall AKA information retrieval, this is the practice of returning to the same topic several times over a period of days, weeks or months in order to strengthen learning of that topic.

Why is recall important?

1 By returning to material and testing understanding you are reinforcing your learning and cementing that knowledge not just for the short term but for the longer term too.

2 By constantly checking your knowledge, you can focus more time on the things that you are struggling to understand or retain, thus making your revision ever more efficient.

How do I incorporate recall into my revision?

There are a number of different techniques which can help you build recall into your revision strategy – here are a few common approaches to get you started.

The 'blank page' method – the simplest method of recall is to write down everything you know about a subject or topic you've studied on a blank piece of paper. Brainstorm everything you can remember, then go back to your notes and quickly check how much you recalled. Then schedule some time to work on the bits you missed. Depending on your preferences you may prefer to brainstorm in a sketch or out loud rather than producing linear notes or bullet points – just experiment with what works for you.

Linear A way of recording information in a sequence. When referring to note-taking, relates to a list of written points taken from a lecture or textbook without any organisation taking place at the same time.

Questions, questions – another very effective technique is to use past papers or sample questions to test your knowledge of a topic. If you don't have these available, write your own questions – this is another great way of thinking about how you'll be asked about things in the exam.

Blank page method An approach to testing your understanding by quickly writing down everything you can recall about a particular topic, allowing you to identify weaker areas that need further work.

Flashcards – a popular variation of the 'questions' approach is to use flashcards. When you're revising a particular topic, write a question on one side of the card, and the answer on the other. When you can answer all the questions, flip the cards around so that you see the answer and have to come up with the question. One advantage of flashcards is that they're highly portable – even a short bus journey or a gap between appointments can be transformed into a high-quality study session.

Incorporating recall into your revision is a very simple but extremely effective step and can be the difference between memorizing something in the short term and actually knowing it for the long term.

Flashcards A popular way of memorizing information and testing recall, the method involves testing yourself with questions written on one side of a card, then checking the answer written on the reverse. Can be done electronically or using physical index cards.

Go beyond the notes

One problem with traditional revision methods such as re-reading and writing out notes is that they tend to represent a relatively shallow approach to revision – OK (although not great) for memorizing facts or details, but not much beyond that. But exams will often require you to do more than simply memorize material – you'll often be expected to *apply* the ideas to practical situations, to *analyse* why and how something occurs, or to *synthesize* different ideas and come to some sort of position. So your revision should be built around these higher order activities – application, analysis, synthesis and evaluation.

That is, you need to practise explaining and describing ideas in detail and with analytical depth. Taking a critical approach to the material you are learning is crucial. This means not simply accepting as fact everything you encounter but instead critiquing the material so that you understand not just the 'what' but also the 'how', as well as being able to recognize weaknesses or counterarguments. You should ask yourself lots of questions about the material, and about your understanding of and engagement with the ideas or arguments.

Analyse Examine something closely so that you can explain it more effectively.

Synthesize To combine elements to make a whole.

Learn something in multiple ways

There are a number of simple strategies you could put in place to start learning and processing material in multiple ways.

You might, for example, look to turn linear notes into a concept map, or do the reverse and verbally describe a picture or diagram, elaborating on what you see in front of you.

Another useful technique is to pretend you're teaching the subject to a class – be sure to actually speak out loud as you explain the idea or concept, perhaps also using a whiteboard or piece of paper to illustrate as you go.

Finally, they're not for everyone but many people can find study groups enormously helpful. So long as you don't get distracted from the task at hand, a study group can be a great way of explaining, elaborating and retrieving ideas and information. Throw questions at each other, teach each other, argue, debate and disagree, and watch your learning grow and grow.

Concept or mind map
A method of visually organising your material around a specific idea or concept that then branches out into specific topics.

'Now that I use a variety of active approaches to study, not only do I feel my learning is improving, I've fallen back in love with my subject again.'

This is a great example of the way in which experimenting and finding out a combination of things that work for you can make a huge difference not only to how well you understand your subject but also how much you start to enjoy it all again. So which techniques will you try?

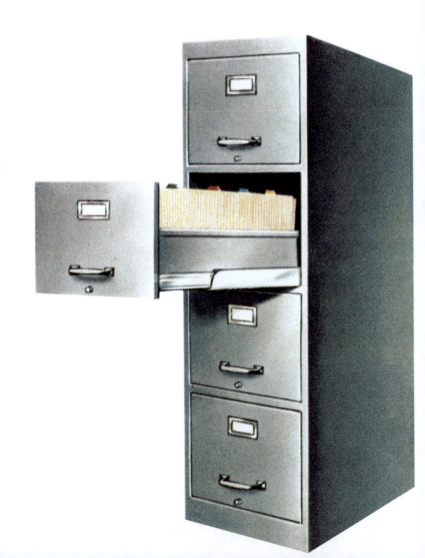

 **CHECK POINT** Get active with your revision

Put a check against each of these active approaches to revision which you think might work for you:

 The 'blank page' method.

 Past papers/sample papers.

 Write your own questions.

 Flashcards.

 Teach a topic.

 Study group/partner.

Other ideas ...

Congratulations

Well done – you've identified and overcome the distractions that may have caused you to procrastinate in the past, you've thought about some of your past approaches to revision that might not have been entirely effective and you've adopted proven techniques that work for you. You're well prepared for the exams.

My exam is today.
What should I do?

10 second summary

A little bit of stress on exam day is normal but there are several things you can do on the day to stay in control of the situation.

Most people get nervous on game day itself, but your aim should be to arrive there in peak condition, prepared for the challenge and with a plan in place. That means no surprises – you know where you're going, how you're going to get there, and what you're going to do when you arrive.

Knowing exactly what you're going to do when the starting pistol is fired will also help you feel in control. Following the suggestions in this book should mean that you arrive at the exam confident and ready to do yourself justice. Then it's just a case of putting your plan for that exam into action.

Surviving and thriving on exam day

> 'You can maximize your chances of exam success by having a plan for the day itself.'

By developing a strategy for before, during and after the exam, you are putting yourself in maximum control of the whole process.

Before the exam

There are several things you can do in the moments before your exam begins to get you in the right frame of mind. Here we look at a few of the more important things to bear in mind:

- *Know where and when the exam is taking place* – you should find out as early as possible the venue and time for your exam and check back regularly to ensure there have been no changes to either. You should also make sure you know where to find the venue.

- *Get there in plenty of time (but not TOO early)* – it hopefully goes without saying that you should allow yourself plenty of time to get to the venue, and that you should aim to arrive early. That said, don't arrive *too* early – standing outside for ages is likely to crank up the stress levels, and if the weather is cold or wet, you may feel uncomfortable before you even enter the venue.

- *Take only what you need* – you don't need your folders, laptop or textbooks with you as it's too late to do any serious study and trying to do so will just stress you out. Flick through some flashcards, or review a concept map or two, but leave the books and folders at home.

- *Avoid the pre-exam huddle* – difficult though it may be, try to avoid discussing what you studied. Everybody has different ideas of what will be in an exam and everyone studies in their own way, so comparing notes is likely to do nothing for you except increase your doubts and raise your stress levels.

Your goal in the final minutes before you go into any exam should be to stay as calm and positive as possible. That allows you to tackle the important bit in the right frame of mind…

During the exam

Perhaps the single most important element of exam strategy – and the one you have most control over – is how you manage your time. Let's think about some of the keys to taking control and managing the clock to your benefit:

- *Take a watch* – although every exam venue should have at least one clock which is visible to you, it still pays to have a watch on your desk so you can keep an eye on the time. If you don't normally use a watch you may want to get hold of one – a basic, bottom-of-the-range model will do the job.

- *Know your timings beforehand* – you should go into every exam with a concrete game plan, including an idea of the time you have to tackle each question and what order you intend to tackle them in. Whatever the format of the exam, knowing your strategy beforehand will give you much more control over the whole process.

- *Stick to your plan* – once you've settled on your strategy, it's crucial that you stick to it. It can be tempting to spend longer on questions you know a lot about, but that always involves spending less time on something else. You should aim to complete all the answers required, and you should be testing your timings out in the final stages of your revision. But in the exam itself, you should always stick to your timings, even if that sometimes means providing a briefer answer than you might otherwise have given.

- *Leave a little time for review* – when considering timings, it's a good idea to leave a little time to go over your answers and look for any obvious errors. This is particularly important in essay-type exams, where even just tidying up grammatical and spelling errors can gain you a few extra marks, but still it's a useful habit to get into in all types of exam.

A student told us

'Rule number one – work on your timings so you get through all the questions you're required to complete.'

After the exam

There are also a couple of things you can do after your exam(s) to make the revision process as effective and stress-free as possible:

- *Avoid exam post-mortems* – at the end of an exam, it's quite natural that people ask each other how it went and discuss their own answers. However, this can be a source of unnecessary anxiety – just because someone gave a different answer to you, it doesn't mean they're right and you're wrong.

- *Forget it* – once you've stepped out of the exam hall, stop thinking about that exam. There is absolutely nothing more you can do to change the outcome anyway. This is particularly important if you still have other exams to take – your focus should be 100% on these exams, not on one you can no longer do anything about.

How well prepared are you for your exam?

☐ Do you know the date, time and venue for each exam?

☐ Have you worked out how to get to the venue, and how to make sure you arrive in plenty of time?

☐ Do you know exactly what is required of you in each exam? What's the format? How many questions do you need to tackle?

☐ Have you worked out a strategy, including approximate timings, for approaching each exam? Have you practised that strategy as part of your revision process?

I've got resits. What should I do now?

10 second summary

Resits are not the end of the world – in fact they're an opportunity to reflect on what went wrong, to develop a more effective approach, and to do yourself justice.

There is no shame in failing an exam. Most of us have done it at one time or another! The most important thing is to learn from the experience, to reflect on why it happened and to take positive action towards the resit opportunity.

It may well be that small changes to your approach can have big results, and that's the value of going through the reflective process. Armed with that reflection and with the tips and techniques outlined throughout this book, you can go about adjusting your approach for any resits you may have. In that way, you can turn a negative experience into a very positive one.

The road to resit success

Paradoxically, future success begins by looking back on why you've been unsuccessful in the past. Before you can start to work more effectively towards your resits, you need to identify what's not worked well, so that you can avoid repeating the same ineffective habits.

A student told us

'Failing my first year exams was a blessing in disguise – it motivated me to take stock and change my whole attitude and approach. I've never looked back since.'

'Why did I fail my exam?'

Below, we list some of the common factors which can cause poor exam performance.

The first few are related to how you study:

- Not enough time spent on revision.

- Ineffective approach to revision.

- Not knowing what to study or where to start.

- Disorganized revision.

There are also a number of common reasons for things going wrong on the day:

- Not answering all the questions or running out of time.

- Overly descriptive answers and lack of analysis.

- Not answering the question asked.

- Leaving the exam early.

- Feeling overly anxious or your mind going blank.

Do any of those sound familiar to you? Were they the hurdles that you couldn't quite clear first time round?

Check your performance

Take a few minutes to think carefully about possible reasons for why you failed your exam(s). Give an honest answer to each one.

What approach did you take to your revision?

....

....

....

....

Suggestion: A different approach might be more effective. **Look again at Section 5.**

Did you allow enough time for revision?

....

....

....

....

Suggestion: Perhaps you started your revision too late, took a cramming approach or just relied on an all-nighter before your exam. What will you do differently this time around? **Look again at Section 4.**

How well organized was your revision schedule?

....

....

....

....

Suggestion: Perhaps you concentrated too much on some areas – possibly the ones you like most – and not enough on others. **Look again at Section 3.**

How did you feel when you were sitting your exams? Did you run out of time or leave the exam early?

....

....

....

....

Suggestion: Perhaps you felt overly anxious or too tired to think clearly. **Look again at Section 6.**

Did you feel you'd done well at the end of the exam? Were your results surprising to you?

....

....

....

....

Suggestion: What will you differently this time around? Read on, and don't forget to go back and read over other relevant sections of this book that can help you put your plans into action!

Get 'under starters orders' again

Assessment in higher education is structured to allow you to demonstrate your learning, and exams are there to provide opportunities to do just that – not as a stick to beat you with! So think about your resits as an opportunity – and go for it!

Practical Tip: If you're finding it hard to stop feeling down, there are techniques you can try to help you feel more positive:

- *Get out and about and spend time away from your desk* – go and see friends, take a walk or spend half an hour reading something different from your revision notes.

- *Give your brain a change of pace* – you may also have heard about mindfulness or meditation. There may be sessions offered at your university that you can join, perhaps offered through student services or your students' association. Take a friend along and have fun as well as learning how to relax more effectively.

Moving on

Once you've identified what you think are your key reasons for failing in the past, you should go back and work through the appropriate sections in this book. In fact, we'd recommend you work through ALL of the sections, regardless of the reason(s) you identified for failing your exams. They won't take long to get through, and they should put you in a much better position to enjoy exam success in the future.

By following all these steps, you should have:

- *An awareness of where things have gone wrong in the past*. You may not yet have all the answers but you should at least have some ideas about things you've been doing which have been ineffective or damaging to your chances of exam success; and how to change those behaviours.

- *Awareness of more effective approaches to learning*. You should now be more aware of how you learn best, as well as recognizing approaches which don't suit you so well. Concentrate on the revision techniques that work for you and avoid those which haven't been so effective in your case.

- *A much more organized revision plan*. If you've followed the advice in the previous sections, you should now find yourself with a revision plan which is realistic, achievable, and firmly focused on what you need to do to pass your resit(s).

- *A more focused approach to revision sessions*. Finally, you should also now have a much sharper idea of what you want to achieve in individual study sessions. Rather than hoping that your brain somehow picks out and retains the key information, you should now be armed with strategies to ensure that, each time you sit down to study, your focus is on precisely that key information and that you're wasting little or no time on information you already know, or don't need.

If you don't yet feel you're at the stage of any of the above, take a little more time to go back over the relevant sections one more time.

Be prepared for future success!

- Take control and plan your exam strategy.

- You will probably need to register for your resits – and potentially pay an administration fee – so deal with this now.

- Take careful note of the venue as resit exams can often be held in different places from those you might be familiar with – find out now how to locate the room on the day.

- What do you picture when you think about your exams? What image pops into your head when you contemplate the amount of revision you have to do? Visualize winning the game by turning these images into pictures of success. This is a technique which is often used by very successful sports people.

- Look after yourself. Get enough sleep, stay hydrated and continue to take regular breaks in between study periods. All-nighters and cramming sessions are not the ticket to resit success.

- Believe in yourself. Remember that by getting to university you are already a successful learner.

'Failure is only failure if you fail to learn from it.'

My exams are over. What next?

10 second summary

Once your exams are finished it's easy to forget all about them. But there are a few things you can do to build on the experience for next time.

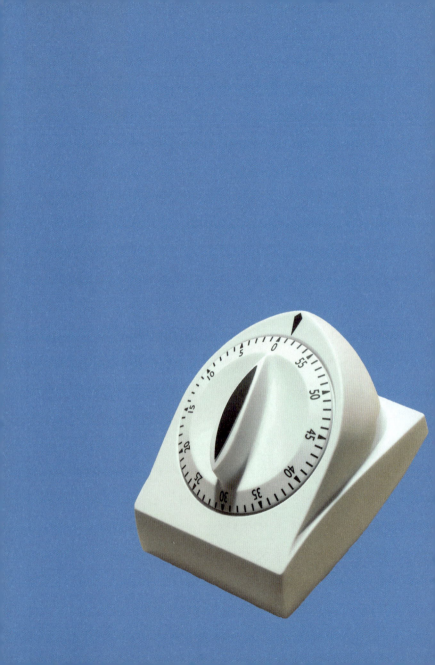

After the full-time whistle, it's important that you give yourself a little bit of space. You should recognize your achievement in successfully navigating a challenging time in any student's year. How are you going to reward yourself for all your hard work?

But before you forget about them completely, take just a little time to reflect on the experience. What went well? What will you do differently next time? Is there anything you need to work on? Taking this time to reflect and think forward to your future exams is all part of the process of winning the exam game.

Congratulations!

Great. Well done. You've worked your way through this book, you've changed (forever) how you work, becoming much more effective, and you've passed your exams. You should celebrate, relax and reward your success!

Things now return to normal. However, also take some time to reflect carefully so that when the new academic year begins, you can slot right back into your chosen degree pathway, and you'll be good to go.

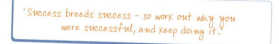

'Success breeds success – so work out why you were successful, and keep doing it.'

ACTIVITY

What good things did you do to revise effectively and keep stress levels at bay?

Make a note of all the things you did to help you get to exam success, so that you can revisit them again next year.

....

....

....

....

If you had any resits, why was this?

Did your choice of subject or course contribute to your problems? Are you choosing the right modules for the right reasons? These are things you may want to discuss with your academic or careers adviser at the start of the new academic year.

....

....

....

....

Are you more confident now?

Why is that? How can you retain – and build on – that confidence for next time around?

....

....

....

....

The skills and techniques you've picked up from this book will stand you in good stead, and your exam success should reinforce your confidence for next time around, so take a few moments to really acknowledge all the good things you incorporated into your exam and revision approach.

A student told us

'I feel much more positive about my future at university now. I have revision strategies and techniques at my fingertips and I know that I can do it – I will pass all those exams next time around!'

Not quite a full medal table?

Perhaps you passed some of your exams but may have had some resits, and you didn't quite make the medal table for those this time around. If you pass some but not all of your exams, you may be allowed to advance to the next year of study whilst 'carrying' the failed module(s) or course(s). Whether or not you can do this depends on a number of factors, not least to do with regulations:

- If you find yourself in this position get in touch with your academic adviser as soon as possible.

- Carrying modules or courses can let you progress but results in a significantly increased workload which can have an adverse effect on the other modules you are taking.

Listen carefully to the advice that you're given and discuss the pros and cons of 'carrying' extra commitment and study forward in this way. Failing some of your exams may feel bad now but it will not define the rest of your life. You will always have choices.

Going for gold next time

Similarly, you might have passed all of your exams this time but feel that you'd like to target even better marks in the future. There are a few questions you can ask yourself which can help you work towards this goal:

- What did I do well?

- What will I definitely do again next time?

- What do I need to do in order to move up to the next grade band (information on what is required to achieve each grade band should be available on your university's website and/or in your course handbook – if you can't find it, ask your adviser or course tutor)?

- Why did I get the mark I got? This can be difficult to establish, but try to think about how effectively you answered the questions, how analytical you were (if applicable) and whether you did each question justice. It may also be possible for you to view or receive some feedback on your exam paper, depending on the regulations in your institution.

- What do I still need to become better at doing? (e.g. you may feel your revision timetable could have been more focused, your revision techniques more varied, or your nerves more under control on the day of the exam).

ACTIVITY A postcard to the future you

Write a postcard to the future you who is preparing for the next set of exams. Make the language positive and encouraging. Congratulate yourself on the success you've enjoyed this time around, and remind your future self of all the progress you have made, all the good stuff you did this time around (you might need two postcards but hey, that's OK – we're celebrating success after all). Address it to yourself and keep it somewhere safe. When the time arrives, dig it out and remind yourself of all the positivity and optimism you were feeling right now. And that should super-boost your confidence as you start preparing for that next exam diet.

Right, enough reflecting. Well done – you've planned effectively, revised successfully, and done your absolute best in the exams. Time to go away and reward yourself. Until next time…

Final checklist: How to know you are done

If you've worked your way through this book, you should be well placed to face future exam challenges with confidence. Use this checklist to make sure you've taken all the necessary steps for exam success.

Have you:

Identified the type(s) of exam you'll be facing?........................... Yes / No

Faced up to the inevitable exam stress by taking
control of the process? .... Yes / No

Created a revision timetable which is focused
and realistic? .... Yes / No

Created an approach to working which minimizes
distractions and reduces procrastination?.................................. Yes / No

Identified potentially ineffective revision techniques and
replaced them with proven approaches? .... *Yes / No*

Developed a strategy which leaves you in control on the
day of the exam? .... *Yes / No*

If you have resits, reflected on where things went wrong and
adapted your approach to maximize your chances of success
in the resits? .... *Yes / No*

Reflected on the strengths and weaknesses of your approach
this time, and thought about how you will approach
future exams? .... *Yes / No*

Glossary

Active vs passive learning   Active learning refers to revision techniques which require you to 'do' something with the material rather than simply re-reading or re-writing.

Analyse   Examine something closely so that you can explain it more effectively.

Blank page method   An approach to testing your understanding by quickly writing down everything you can recall about a particular topic, allowing you to identify weaker areas that need further work.

Concept or mind map   A method of visually organising your material around a specific idea or concept that then branches out into specific topics.

Decluttering   The practice, when studying, of gathering only the materials you need for any one study session, rather than being surrounded by books and notes that you do not need at that particular moment.

Essay based exam   An exam where you will be required to write a defined number of properly structured essay answers.

Flashcards   A popular way of memorising information and testing recall, the method involves testing yourself with questions written on one side of a card, then checking the answer written on the reverse. Can be done electronically or using physical index cards.

Going 'off the grid'   The practice of avoiding all distractions. Although particularly referring to turning off email and social media notifications, it can also refer to physically removing yourself from a particular environment in order to avoid human distractions.

Interleaving   The practice of mixing up topics and revision activities within a single revision slot.

Linear   A way of recording information in a sequence. When referring to note-taking, relates to a list of written points taken from a lecture or textbook without any organisation taking place at the same time.

Multiple choice questions (MCQs)   A common type of exam where you are given a question and a series of possible answers, from which you must chose the correct response. Likely to involve answering a large number of questions in a relatively short space of time.

Open book exam   An exam where you are allowed to refer to certain material (usually textbooks or notes).

Procrastination   The habit of putting off or avoiding tasks you don't want to do. Particularly prevalent around exam revision time!

Recall   AKA information retrieval, this is the practice of returning to the same topic several times over a period of days, weeks or months in order to strengthen learning of that topic.

Short answer questions (SAQs)   Exam questions which require you to give a short answer. Expectations in terms of structure and style may be less strict than for essay based exams – for example, it may be possible to answer in bullet points or by drawing a diagram.

Spaced practice   This refers to the theory that time allocated to a specific topic will be more productive if split over several revision slots rather than completed in one sitting.

Synthesize   To combine elements to make a whole.

Tapering   The practice of levelling off your revision as the exam approaches so that the last few days are spent reviewing learning rather than in intensive cramming.